The first ever co-production between

**SHERMAN CYMRU**       **Bristol Old Vic**

# BEFORE IT RAINS

## by Katherine Chandler

This production was first performed on
10 September 2012 at Bristol Old Vic

Cyngor Celfyddydau Cymru
Arts Council of Wales

Noddir gan
**Lywodraeth Cymru**
Sponsored by
**Welsh Government**

CARDIFF
CAERDYDD

BRISTOL CITY COUNCIL

Supported by
**ARTS COUNCIL
ENGLAND**

# BEFORE IT RAINS

by Katherine Chandler

## Cast

| | |
|---|---|
| Michael | **Craig Gazey** |
| Gloria | **Lisa Palfrey** |
| Carl | **Harry Ferrier** |

## Creative Team

| | |
|---|---|
| Director | Róisín McBrinn |
| Designer | Alyson Cummins |
| Lighting Designer | Paul Keogan |
| Sound Designer | Simon Slater |
| Sound Assistant | Eamon Walsh |
| Movement Director | Yael Loewenstein |
| Stage Manager | Polly Meech |
| Deputy Stage Manager | Kevin Smith |
| Production Photography | Farrows Creative |
| Publicity Design | Smith & Milton |

*Before It Rains* was originally developed in association with Pentabus Theatre

# A Message from the Writer

My family are from a typical 1950s council estate and I remember a great community of working people who were proud of their estate and had strong community values. The estate I remembered was very open-door, people on doorsteps chatting, kids out and playing and neighbours looking out for each other. I moved back to the same estate after having my daughter and it felt very different.

As a writer I was intrigued as to why that was. At around the same time I watched some documentaries about post-war council estates and there were lots of news stories about class and 'troubled families'. *Before It Rains* explores all of these themes but is essentially a story of a mother's love.

*Katherine Chandler*

# Cast

**Lisa Palfrey** – Gloria

**Theatre credits:** *Canvas* (Chichester Festival Theatre); *The Kitchen Sink* (Bush); *Red Bud, Ingredient X, Under the Blue Sky* (Royal Court); *Small Change, Ghosts* (Sherman Cymru, Cardiff); *Blink* (tour/Off Broadway); *Gathered Dust & Dead Skin* (Live Theatre, Newcastle); *Festen* (West End/Almeida); *The Iceman Cometh* (Almeida); *Cardiff East, Under Milkwood* (National Theatre); *Yerma, Story of an African Farm* (National Theatre Studio); as well as national tours of *House of America* and *Flowers of the Dead Red Sea*.

**Film credits:** *360, Hunky Dory, Guest House Paradiso, House of America, The Deadness of Dad, The Englishman Who Went Up a Hill But Came Down a Mountain, Maybe Baby.*

**Television credits:** *Pen Talar, Blodau, Pobol Y Cwm, Inspector Lynley, The Bill, Outside the Rules, Casualty, Green-Eyed Monster, Split Second, Magistrates, Mind Games, Lord of Misrule, Soldier Soldier.*

**Craig Gazey** – Michael

Craig trained at the Royal Welsh College of Music and Drama.

**Theatre credits:** *Funny Peculiar* (UK tour); *Third Floor* (Trafalgar Studios); *Holding Fire!, The Merchant of Venice* (Shakespeare's Globe); *Antony and Cleopatra, The Tempest, Julius Caesar* (Royal Shakespeare Company); *The Santaland Diaries* (Birmingham Rep); *Cleansed* (Oxford Stage Company); *Harvest* (Royal Court).

**Television credits:** *Coronation Street, The Royal, The Circle, Criminal Justice, The Bill, Caerdydd, 3-7-11.*

Craig recently played Graeme Proctor in ITV's *Coronation Street* for which he won various awards, including Best Newcomer at the 2010 National Television Awards and Best Comedy Actor at the 2010 British Soap Awards.

**Harry Ferrier** – Carl

Harry trained at Royal Academy of Dramatic Art.

**Theatre credits**: *The Radicalisation of Bradley Manning* (National Theatre Wales); *Caravaggio's Head, After the Storm* (Sgript Cymru).

**Film credits:** *House of Boys, Nightwatching, Flick, Calorie.*

**Television credits:** *The Silence, Monroe, Doctor Who, Young Dracula, I Shouldn't Be Alive.*

# Creative Team

**Katherine Chandler** – Writer

Katherine Chandler's first play was a musical comedy called *The Bankrupt Bride* that was produced by Theatr na n'Óg in 2009 and toured nationally. She has had a long-standing relationship with the company and her play *We Need Bees*, a children's play for the under-sevens, is currently on tour. As a writer, she has also had short plays produced by Dirty Protest and Spectacle Theatre. In 2011 one of her plays was selected by Pentabus Theatre as their We Are Here 2011 winning script and was developed in association with Sherman Cymru. Katherine is the recipient of an Arts Council Wales grant to write a new female-led comedy and is under commission from National Theatre Wales to develop a new piece of work with them. In early 2013 Katherine will be on a studio attachment at the National Theatre (England).

**Róisín McBrinn** – Director

Róisín is Associate Director at Sherman Cymru.

**Theatre includes:** *Yellow Moon* (Rustaveli Theatre, Georgia); *Sixty-Six Books* (Bush); *Yerma* (West Yorkshire Playhouse); *Novecento* (Donmar Warehouse, Trafalgar Studios); *No Escape, Perve* (Abbey, Dublin); *Cityscape* (Sherman Cymru); *Crestfall* (Theatre503); *Sleeping Beauty* (Helix, Dublin); *The Field* (Tricycle); *Whereabouts* (Fishamble Theatre Company); *A Thousand Yards* (Southwark Playhouse); *References to Salvador Dalí Make Me Hot, Gompers* (Arcola).

Róisín was the Donmar's Resident Assistant Director in 2003, won the Young Vic/Jerwood Young Director's Award in 2004 and was the recipient of the Quercus Award 2010 run by the National Theatre. She was resident at the National Theatre Studio in 2009.

**Alyson Cummins** – Designer

**Set and costume theatre design includes:** *Pornography* (Waking Exploits); *Ruben Guthrie* (Iron Bark); *How the World Began* (Arcola); *The Yellow Wallpaper* (Dublin Fringe Festival); *Hamlet* (Second Age); *Colleen Bawn* Project (Project/Civic/Bedrock); *Serious Money, Dying City* (Rough Magic SEEDS); *Extremities* (Spark to a Flame); *Crosswired* (East London Dance Festival); *The Trials of Brother Jero, Through a Film Darkly* (Arambe); *Daily Bread* (DYT); *Top Girls* (Galloglass); *Forget-Me-Not Lane* (Teatro Technis); *Ya Get Me* (Old Vic Education Department).

**Set design includes:** *Perve, No Escape* (Abbey, Dublin); *The Trailer of Bridget Dinnigan* (ITM); *Off Plan* (RAW).

Alyson studied architecture at University College Dublin, after which she was awarded an Arts Council grant to train at Motley Theatre design course and was a finalist in the biennial Linbury Prize for Stage Design in 2007.

**Paul Keogan** – Lighting Designer

Paul studied Drama at Trinity College Dublin and Glasgow University.

**Theatre includes:** *A Streetcar Named Desire, Tartuffe* (Liverpool Playhouse); *A Woman of No Importance, Da, Molly Sweeney, The Birds, Festen, Performances, Gates of Gold* (Gate, Dublin); *Big Maggie, Penelope, The Walworth Farce* (Druid, Galway); *Novecento* (Trafalgar Studios); *Curse of the Starving Class, The Resistible Rise of Arturo Ui* (Abbey, Dublin); *Ages of the Moon* (Abbey, Dublin/Atlantic Theatre NYC), *Boss Grady's Boys* (Gaiety Theatre, Dublin); *Intemperance* (Liverpool Everyman); *The Taming of the Shrew* (Royal Shakespeare Company); *Harvest* (Royal Court); *The Stock Da'Wa, Born Bad* (Hampstead); *Blue/Orange* (Crucible, Sheffield); *The Crucible* (Regent's Park); *Angel/Babel* (Operating Theatre, Dublin); *Trad* (Galway Arts Festival); *Man of Aran, Re-imagined* (Once Off Productions, Ireland).

**Simon Slater** – Sound Designer

**Theatre includes:** *Constellations* (Royal Court); *Nor A* (Belgrade Theatre, Coventry); *Death of a Salesman, The Grouch, Treasure Island, James and the Giant Peach, The Wind in the Willows, Heroes* (Watermill, Newbury); *No Naughty Bits, As You Like It, Enlightenment* (Hampstead); *The Lady and the Van* (national tour); *The Deep Blue Sea* (West Yorkshire Playhouse); *Fatherland* (Gate, London); *Two Men of Florence* (Huntington); *Romeo and Juliet, Henry V, Julius Caesar* (Royal Shakespeare Company); *Cling to Me Like Ivy* (Birmingham Rep); *Kafka's Dick* (Watford Palace); *James and the Giant Peach* (Octagon, Bolton); *Coyote on a Fence* (Manchester Royal Exchange/Duchess); *Beachy Head, Mile End* (Analogue); *Peter Pan, The Wizard of Oz* (Winchester Theatre Royal); *Honour* (Wyndham's); *Road Movie* (Library, Manchester); *Writer's Block* (Nuffield, Southampton); *Macbeth* (Albery).

**Yael Loewenstein** – Movement Director

**Theatre includes:** *Tess of the d'Urbervilles* (South Hill Park); *Korczac* (Rose, Kingston); *Yerma* (West Yorkshire Playhouse); *Much Ado About Nothing* (Theatre Royal, Bury St Edmunds); *Scheherazade* (Bradford Playhouse); *Fool's Gold* (Barbican, Plymouth); *The Firebird, 101 Dalmations, The Lady and the Lion, The Wind in the Willows, Peter Pan, Oliver!, Hiawatha, Bugsy Malone, Oh! What a Lovely War, A Midsummer Night's Dream* (NLCS); *Adult Child/Dead Child* (Edinburgh Fringe/Unicorn); *The Wind in the Willows* (Regent's Park); *The Skin of Our Teeth* (assistant choreographer, Young Vic); *Over Gardens Out* (Southwark Playhouse); *The Blood of Others* (Arcola); *Pericles* (GSA); *A Midsummer Night's Dream, Macbeth* (London South Bank University).

Yael also works in dance, opera and motion-capture for video games.

**Polly Meech** – Stage Manager

Polly trained at the Bristol Old Vic Theatre School.

**Theatre credits include:** Shakespeare at the Tobacco Factory, Bristol Old Vic, Tobacco Factory Theatre, Regent's Park Open Air Theatre, Young Vic, Royal Court, Nuffield Theatre, Salisbury Playhouse.

**Kevin Smith** – Deputy Stage Manager

Kevin trained at the Royal Welsh College of Music and Drama.

**Theatre credits include:** The Society of British Theatre Designers, Oxford Playhouse, Volcano Theatre Company, Theatr na n'Óg, Hijinx Theatre, Sherman Cymru, National Theatre Wales, Notional Theatre.

## *Before It Rains* in rehearsal

Photography by Farrows Creative

# SHERMAN CYMRU

At Sherman Cymru we aim to make and present great theatre that is ambitious, inventive and memorable for our audiences and to create strong, responsive and enriching relationships with our communities. We produce work in both English and Welsh and tour widely within Wales and the UK.

Sherman Cymru, Senghennydd Road, Cardiff CF24 4YE, *tel* 029 2064 6900
**www.shermancymru.co.uk**

# Bristol Old Vic

At Bristol Old Vic we aim to create a programme which engages with and reflects the vitality, variety and vibrancy of our extraordinary city. Bristol, quite simply, is incredible; rich in history, heritage, cyclists, cider, endless invention and a bursting brook of rule breaking artistic and cultural wonderfulness. We hope to contribute to all of the above by building relationships and working with artists, audiences, spaces and places to create world-class theatre and performance that a city like Bristol deserves.

# BEFORE IT RAINS

Katherine Chandler

Before It Rains *is dedicated to the memory of my sons*
*Osian Peter O'Donnell and Iwan Hedd O'Donnell*

*And to*
*Guy, Mali and Mathonwy*

'The Law of the Jungle'
from *The Jungle Book*
by Rudyard Kipling

Now this is the Law of the Jungle –
as old and as true as the sky;
And the Wolf that shall keep it may prosper,
but the Wolf that shall break it must die.

As the creeper that girdles the tree-trunk
the Law runneth forward and back –
For the strength of the Pack is the Wolf,
and the strength of the Wolf is the Pack.

Wash daily from nose-tip to tail-tip;
drink deeply, but never too deep;
And remember the night is for hunting,
and forget not the day is for sleep.

The Jackal may follow the Tiger,
but, Cub, when thy whiskers are grown,
Remember the Wolf is a Hunter –
go forth and get food of thine own.

Keep peace with Lords of the Jungle –
the Tiger, the Panther, and Bear.
And trouble not Hathi the Silent,
and mock not the Boar in his lair.

When Pack meets with Pack in the Jungle,
and neither will go from the trail,
Lie down till the leaders have spoken –
it may be fair words shall prevail.

When ye fight with a Wolf of the Pack,
ye must fight him alone and afar,
Lest others take part in the quarrel,
and the Pack be diminished by war.

The Lair of the Wolf is his refuge,
and where he has made him his home,
Not even the Head Wolf may enter,
not even the Council may come.

The Lair of the Wolf is his refuge,
but where he has digged it too plain,
The Council shall send him a message,
and so he shall change it again.

If ye kill before midnight, be silent,
and wake not the woods with your bay,
Lest ye frighten the deer from the crop,
and your brothers go empty away.

Ye may kill for yourselves, and your mates,
and your cubs as they need, and ye can;
But kill not for pleasure of killing,
and seven times never kill Man!

If ye plunder his Kill from a weaker,
devour not all in thy pride;
Pack-Right is the right of the meanest;
so leave him the head and the hide.

The Kill of the Pack is the meat of the Pack.
Ye must eat where it lies;
And no one may carry away of that meat to his lair,
or he dies.

The Kill of the Wolf is the meat of the Wolf.
He may do what he will;
But, till he has given permission,
the Pack may not eat of that Kill.

Cub-Right is the right of the Yearling.
From all of his Pack he may claim
Full-gorge when the killer has eaten;
and none may refuse him the same.

Lair-Right is the right of the Mother.
From all of her year she may claim
One haunch of each kill for her litter,
and none may deny her the same.

Cave-Right is the right of the Father –
to hunt by himself for his own:
He is freed of all calls to the Pack;
he is judged by the Council alone.

Because of his age and his cunning,
because of his gripe and his paw,
In all that the Law leaveth open,
the word of your Head Wolf is Law.

Now these are the Laws of the Jungle,
and many and mighty are they;
But the head and the hoof of the Law
and the haunch and the hump is – Obey!

## Acknowledgements

Kate Budgen

Róisín McBrinn

John E. McGrath

Sian Summers, Sharon Clark

Lisa Palfrey, Craig Gazey, Harry Ferrier, Helen Griffin,
Matthew Aubrey, Garnon Davies and Rhi Richards

Dr Judith Gurry

**Characters**

MICHAEL

CARL

GLORIA

**Note on the Text**

*Scenes One, Six and Nine have no dialogue. I imagine the
action within the scenes to be choreographed movement
influenced by animal behaviour and ritual. When appropriate,
elements of this movement should be used and repeated
throughout all scenes.*

*Michael is a man with high-functioning Asperger syndrome (not
diagnosed) and routine and repetition are important for his
character. Michael likes his food and will have a carrier bag of
goodies at all times. Michael's digging is a way of him
regulating himself from sensory over/underload so should be
used sensitively alongside his emotions.*

*Gloria is a heavy drinker and throughout the play will be at
varying stages of intoxication from sober to drunk and anything
inbetween.*

*Carl is around and watching throughout most of the scenes. He
uses a ball and particularly a ball-bounce as his calling card.*

*This text went to press before the end of rehearsals and so may
differ slightly from the play as performed.*

**Scene One**

*Tuesday, midday.*

MICHAEL *is centre stage eating a sandwich out of a carrier bag.*

*A football is being bounced. We hear the noise of the bounce before we see what it is.*

CARL *appears, bouncing the football. He notices* MICHAEL.

*Approaches* MICHAEL *still bouncing the ball. Circles him. Still bouncing.*

MICHAEL *eats his sandwich.*

CARL *watches.*

*Intrigued.*

CARL *appears behind him, holding the ball. Says nothing.*

*Watches* MICHAEL.

MICHAEL *smiles as he eats open-mouthed, an attempt to make friends.* CARL *watches him.* MICHAEL *stops smiling. Carries on eating. More self-conscious now.*

CARL *stands next to* MICHAEL *like soldiers on parade.*

*Copies every movement – hand to mouth. Hand to mouth. Bites the sandwich. Bites the sandwich. Chews. Chews.* MICHAEL *carries on chewing.* CARL *mimics him comically. Laughs. Menacing? Maybe not.* MICHAEL *smiles.*

CARL *grabs the sandwich from* MICHAEL.

CARL *laughs.*

MICHAEL *laughs.*

CARL *stops laughing.*

**Scene Two**

*Wednesday, late afternoon.*

*A deserted allotment.*

MICHAEL *digging.*

GLORIA. *Not dressed to work. Pottering. Pours herself a coffee from a flask.*

*She puts a shot in her coffee. Another for luck.*

GLORIA *sways, sings 'Que Sera, Sera'. Not comical. Lost a little. A moment of contentment. The sun shines. She breathes in the fresh air. Forget your troubles.*

MICHAEL *digs.*

GLORIA *sits on an old deckchair and picks up a gardening magazine, starts to flick through.*

*A cloud passes over them.* GLORIA *looks up at the cloud.*

MICHAEL. Cumulus. Water vapour and dust. The cauliflower cloud. It's gonna rain.

GLORIA. Shut up, Michael.

> *She puts the magazine over her head and leans back on the chair.*

MICHAEL. The clouds hold on to the water droplets until they're too heavy. Gravity makes 'em fall. It's gonna rain.

GLORIA. We'll put some roses in. Brighten the allotment up.

> MICHAEL *digs.*

Not the white ones.

MICHAEL. Look like shit.

GLORIA. Petals go brown.

*She takes a swig of her coffee. Starts flicking through a
gardening brochure from the magazine.*

MICHAEL *digs.*

We'll go up the garden centre later. (*Reading off the
brochure.*) Look at this, Michael, it says here you can buy
garden art. Art for your garden. Have you ever heard of...
oh, look! It's a sheep made of wire. And just by here. There's
a lizard you can put on your wall. Made of wire like the
sheep.

*She drains her coffee.*

Hey, Michael, there's a lot of that garden art already on the
estate.

MICHAEL. Is there?

GLORIA. That lot that moved into No. 22 got a fridge on the
front garden. There we go. That's garden art for you, right
there outside No. 22.

GLORIA *laughs.*

And the man with the van next to Mr Singh, he got a burnt-
out telly on his.

GLORIA *laughs.*

That's garden art estate-style, aye, Michael.

MICHAEL *looks to the clouds.*

MICHAEL. It's gonna rain.

GLORIA. So you said.

MICHAEL. It's the cauliflower cloud.

GLORIA. Thank you, Michael Fish.

MICHAEL. Soil, is an earthly compound made of living and
non-living matter that is formed in several layers over
millions of years.

GLORIA *puts down the brochure. Pours herself another drink. This time starts with shots, adds coffee as an afterthought.*

MICHAEL *digs.*

GLORIA. Got a face on you again, Michael.

MICHAEL. Haven't.

GLORIA. Don't tell me 'haven't'. I'm the unlucky sod who gotta look at it day and night.

MICHAEL. Don't look at it then.

GLORIA. You're a miserable sod.

GLORIA *looks at next door's allotment.*

MICHAEL. Rain makes soil.

GLORIA. She got a climbing rose.

MICHAEL. Rocks get bigger when the weather gets hot. The weather gets cold, rocks get smaller. This happens often enough, the rocks crack and break up into small pieces that break into even smaller pieces. They gets really small they turns into soil. Rain gets into rocks and breaks them apart. It makes soil. Rain.

GLORIA. I said, Michael. Celia Lynch. She only gone an' got herself a rose, Michael. A climbing one. Yellow.

MICHAEL *stops digging.*

MICHAEL. Looks like shit.

GLORIA. That's a begonia! She've got a climbing rose and a begonia. Both yellow.

MICHAEL. Both looks like shit.

GLORIA. Beautiful they are. Just stood there in their pots. Blowing a bit. All puffed up and proud.

I fancy they think they're better than the rest of us.

*Watches the flowers a bit.*

And they're right. Cos they are. They're beautiful.

I used to be beautiful, Michael.

I was bloody gorgeous in my day. Drop-dead I was.

MICHAEL. Drop-dead ugly.

GLORIA. Talking about yourself again.

MICHAEL. Talking 'bout you.

GLORIA. We'll get some. Some begonias.

MICHAEL. This soil's no good for flowers. It's like clay.

GLORIA. Is that right?

MICHAEL. I know about soil.

GLORIA. You would.

MICHAEL. Plants needs soil to root themselves and grow.

This is clay loam. You got to treat it right then you won't have no problems. We need grit or heavy sand. I can dig it in.

GLORIA. You can do that all right.

MICHAEL. Grit or heavy sand.

GLORIA. So you said.

MICHAEL. Sand has to be grainy.

GLORIA. Sand is grainy, y'daft sod.

MICHAEL. Not soft sand. We don't want soft sand. A uniform sand is no good for our purpose.

GLORIA. Boring me, Michael.

MICHAEL. There's more confusion regarding sand than any other of the aggregates. It's all to do with the grading. You got to get the right grain size.

GLORIA (*drains her cup*). It's all about the size, Michael.

MICHAEL. We'll grow some vegetables.

GLORIA. You're so sodding boring.

MICHAEL. Once I gets the soil right. Can grow all sorts.

GLORIA. All sorts, aye?

MICHAEL. All sorts.

GLORIA. Can you grow me a new man, Michael? Can you do that for your mam? Tall and handsome with big muscles and hands as big as spades.

MICHAEL. Get the right compost.

GLORIA. Is it that easy, is it? Get the right compost and grow the right man.

MICHAEL. Grow vegetables with the right compost.

GLORIA. Always thinking of your stomach, you. Like that thing, that what'sitcalled in that film. 'Feed me,' you know the one. That's you, Michael, that is. 'Feed me,' go on, Michael, do it, 'Feed me.'

MICHAEL. No.

GLORIA. Go on, son, 'Feed me,' like that thing, that Triffid thing off the film.

MICHAEL. No, I don't want to.

GLORIA (*mimics*). 'I don't want to.' Christ, Michael, I'm only after a bit of fun. (*Mimics*.) 'No, I don't want to.' Shut up then, stop boring me.

*Pours herself a drink. This time no coffee.*

Bit of fun, that's all I wants. Bit of a laugh before I'm too old.

MICHAEL. You are too old.

GLORIA. Before I'm dead.

*MICHAEL starts digging.*

*GLORIA picks up the brochure again.*

*Flicks through it.*

*Boring. Looks around.*

Lisa says the postmen have stopped delivering since that kid with the eye shot Robbie Coles in the leg with a pellet gun, week before last.

MICHAEL. Robbie the postie?

GLORIA. Said he's not worn shorts since and he was doing it in all weathers for charity. Them lads are trouble, Michael. You make sure you keeps out of their way. They already got a name for themselves and they've not been yer a full month.

You know we have to go down Lisa's shop to pick it up now. What's the world coming to, aye, Michael?

MICHAEL. Don't know.

GLORIA. Cos that's the point of post innit, son. That it's posted. Don't know what's going on around yer lately. But it's changed, I'll tell you that for nothing. It's all changed.

You can pop to the shop for me later. Pick me up some fags. Cut through the woods if it's still light.

MICHAEL. If you like.

GLORIA. And don't hang around boring that Lisa when she's working.

MICHAEL. I don't.

GLORIA. You do. She can't get rid of you.

MICHAEL. I don't.

GLORIA. You do.

MICHAEL. I don't.

GLORIA. She goes out with that goon in the chippy. The one with the hat. Keeps saying 'Yes, indeedy.'

MICHAEL. She don't go out with no one.

GLORIA. Don't hang round her, that's all I'm saying.

MICHAEL. I don't.

GLORIA. We don't want no trouble again, Michael.

MICHAEL. I don't want no trouble.

GLORIA. Straight to the shop and back, Michael. You don't know who's hanging around.

MICHAEL. Straight to the shop and back. I'll cut through the woods.

GLORIA. If it's light. I don't like you out in the dark, specially not down them woods.

MICHAEL. I won't go if it's dark, Mam.

GLORIA. I like you home, before tea.

MICHAEL. Gonna take me all night to get this dug.

GLORIA. I'll get us a nice piece of fish for our tea, Michael.

MICHAEL. I needs grit.

GLORIA *gets up and lights a fag.*

GLORIA. Darren from the club'll be able to get us some of that.

MICHAEL. Grit or heavy-grain sand.

GLORIA. He gets all sorts. He'll get it for me if I give him the nod.

I said, Michael, Darren from the club. Do anything for me, that Darren.

MICHAEL. Two bags.

GLORIA. I'll be down the club tonight.

MICHAEL. I can dig it in.

GLORIA. Gonna spend my evening slow-dancing with Darren to the soulful tones of Lionel Ritchie.

MICHAEL. I hate Lionel Ritchie.

GLORIA. You hate everything, you do.

MICHAEL. I hate shit. And Lionel Ritchie's shit.

GLORIA. What do you know about Lionel Ritchie?

MICHAEL. I know he's shit.

GLORIA. I know Darren loves him. Loves to dance with me to him.

MICHAEL. Dances with anyone who's drunk enough.

GLORIA. Shut up you little gobshite.

MICHAEL. Dance with anyone, snog with anyone, sex with anyone.

GLORIA. Sod off. What do you know about it? Cheeky little shit.

MICHAEL. Talk a load of bollocks.

GLORIA. What are you talking about?

MICHAEL. Talking about you talking a load of bollocks.

GLORIA. Shut up. Just you shut your mouth. Cos you don't know nothing so you keep this out – (*Nose*.) an' that shut – (*Mouth*.)

*Stubs her cigarette out furiously on the fence. Catches her finger on the wire.*

Now look what you made me do.

MICHAEL *immediately repentant. Goes to her.*

MICHAEL. Got any TCP?

GLORIA. Yes, you know me, always carry me medical-emergency bag with me.

Course I haven't.

MICHAEL. That's what you need. TCP.

GLORIA. Is it? Is that what I need.

MICHAEL. I'll get you some of them begonias, Mam. We'll ask Mr Singh. He'll get us some from the cash-and-carry.

Your hand, Mam. That's what you need, TCP.

GLORIA. TLC. That's what I need.

MICHAEL. TCP. TCP. TCP. (*Repeats.*)

*Puts her arm around* MICHAEL.

GLORIA. Yes. TCP. Michael.

It's fine. It'll be fine, son. It's just a scratch.

What's that?

MICHAEL *looks over.*

MICHAEL. What?

GLORIA. There by the shed.

MICHAEL. A chair.

GLORIA. It's a lounger. Celia Lynch 'ave got a lounger. A wood one. What wood is that? It's not pine. Is that pine? It'll have cushions, that will. I'd love that. Leaving it out like that on this estate. She'll learn.

MICHAEL. I can get you one of them if you wants one.

GLORIA. Can you now.

MICHAEL. I got a friend.

GLORIA. That's right, you got a friend.

MICHAEL. That's right.

GLORIA. Don't start.

MICHAEL. I got a friend.

GLORIA. What friend have you got?

MICHAEL. You can have that chair, if you wants it.

GLORIA. What are you talking about. Talking shit, Michael. 'That' chair.

MICHAEL. Any chair.

GLORIA. Shut up, Michael.

MICHAEL. My friend can get you a chair.

GLORIA. I don't want a chair. 'That chair.' For Christ's sake.

MICHAEL. My friend can get you any chair you wants.

GLORIA. How can he get me that chair?

MICHAEL. I'll tell him.

GLORIA. You'll tell him nothing cos there is no friend.

MICHAEL. There is a friend.

GLORIA. Who is he then, this friend?

MICHAEL. Just a friend.

GLORIA. I'd know if you had a friend.

MICHAEL. How do you know. You don't know nothing cos you're pissed.

GLORIA. Who'd have you as friend? Tell me?

MICHAEL. I got a friend.

GLORIA. You haven't got no friends so stop talking shit. I don't have to be sober to know that.

MICHAEL. You don't know nothing.

GLORIA. Shut up, Michael.

*A silence.*

MICHAEL *carries on digging. Calm down.*

MICHAEL. I got a friend.

**Scene Three**

*Thursday, early afternoon.*

MICHAEL *and* CARL *sat on a wall.*

MICHAEL *eating food out of a carrier bag.*

CARL. It's all to do with the traditions of combat, Mikey boy. You're basically defeating other persons or defending yourself from other persons fucking with you. It's like a religion, man. It's got a code of honour.

MICHAEL. Like the Scouts.

CARL. Nothing fucking like the Scouts. Are you taking the piss?

MICHAEL. No.

CARL. Martial arts, Mikey, 'the art of warfare'. Nothing like the fucking Scouts. I'm basically a trained warrior. Which is why I would in the correct given situation have to practise three verbal warnings before combat. Like this, see: they would approach me, whatever, maybe they're carrying a weapon, let's say a smashed bottle.

MICHAEL. A Swiss army knife.

CARL. Not a blade, Mikey.

MICHAEL. A machete.

CARL. I'm thinking more random than that. I'm way ahead of you there, mate. A little twat with a small prick, he's the one with the bottle. So I'm gonna kick off cos that's what I do but before I do I say, 'I must warn you, gentlemen, I am trained in the arts of the martial in say tae kwon do.'

MICHAEL. Tae kwon do, a Korean martial art and the national sport of South Korea. Tae kwon do may be loosely translated as 'the art of the foot and fist' or 'the art of kicking and punching'.

CARL. You got it, Mikey boy. But these little fuckers. They
     don't give a fuck. They haven't even heard of it. They're off
     on one, giving it all 'We're gonna fucking kick your head in
     an' all that.' That is when I issue my second warning. And I
     start with a 'number two'. Just so they know. 'Number two, I
     must warn you, gentlemen, I am trained in the arts of the
     martial in ju-jitsu.'

MICHAEL. And tae kwon do?

CARL. Same thing. Now they starts listening. But only a bit,
     cos they're thinking 'Who's this weird fucker giving it
     mouth back at us?' They're thinking 'Why isn't he running
     in that direction?' Now they're getting it. I can see the
     change in their eyes, Mikey boy. And it's at that moment I
     strike with a number three. Same thing, but on the end I kick
     the fuckers halfway into next year.

MICHAEL. What about the bottle?

CARL. Don't fucking think about the bottle, Mikey? The kid
     with the bottle is on the floor with the bottle shoved up his
     arse for his troubles.

     CARL *jumps off the wall. Starts shadow-fighting himself.
     Takes off his coat, punches his own stomach.*

     Hit me here. As hard as you can. Take me by surprise.

MICHAEL. I don't want to.

CARL. Right by here. Hard as you like.

MICHAEL. No.

CARL. By surprise.

MICHAEL. No.

CARL. Get off the fucking wall and take me by surprise.

     MICHAEL *thinks about it. Then reluctantly puts down his
     bag and gets off the wall.* CARL *is prancing around, boxer-
     style.*

MICHAEL. Are we going to the woods, Carl?

CARL. Right here.

MICHAEL. Thought we was going to the woods.

CARL. By surprise. I can take it. As hard as you like.

MICHAEL. I don't want to.

CARL. I'll close my eyes. Just land one on me…

*As he talks,* MICHAEL *punches him full pelt, takes the wind out of him.*

You little fucker. That was too hard. I was talking. You shouldn't hit a man when he's talking. Martial law. And you just broke it.

MICHAEL. Sorry, Carl.

CARL *gathers himself together. Leans back against the wall.* MICHAEL *does the same.*

Are we going up the woods or not, Carl?

CARL. Got things to do, haven't I.

MICHAEL. You said we was going up the woods, said you'd show me how to set the traps, catch some rats.

CARL. Our kid wants me home by two. I'm a busy man, aren't I.

MICHAEL. I'm a busy man.

CARL. You. What you got to do?

MICHAEL. Got my job.

CARL. Pushing trolleys. Call that a job. It's like fucking community service, that is. You even got one of them jackets, haven't you? I seen you in it. One of them bright fuck-off yellow things.

MICHAEL. Superior-quality high-visibility jacket. I got a vest an' all for the summer. Next time though I'm gonna ask for a fleece lining.

CARL. Fucking hell, mate. You needs to get out of that game fast.

MICHAEL. Keeps me busy. Nine to one Monday, Wednesday, Friday.

CARL. Getting pissed on in all weathers. Freezing your tits off. What's the perks? I bet you helps yourself to the produce. Maybes a bit of till-dipping if you're short, like.

MICHAEL. No.

CARL. You could be quids in there, mate. You're missing a trick. No harm in helping yourself to a couple of quid if the opportunity arises. Everyone does it.

MICHAEL. I just does my trolleys and comes home.

CARL. Sounds like a mug's game.

We got better things planned in life, me and our kid.

MICHAEL. It's gonna rain later, Carl. We should go ratting now.

CARL. Got better things to do than hang around here.

MICHAEL. I knows what to do.

CARL. Like today, got urgent business to attend to, today.

MICHAEL. I been ratting before with Mr Singh.

CARL. You knows Leighton Spears, Mikey?

Me an' our kid got urgent business with Leighton Spears.

MICHAEL. Mr Singh brought his Jack Russell. Should've seen him, Carl.

CARL. I bet he was like a fucking rocket going off up the woods, was he?

MICHAEL. Like a rocket he was. Mr Singh was chasing him.

CARL. He wouldn't have caught the little fucker.

MICHAEL. He didn't, Carl. He couldn't catch him. He called him a little shit.

CARL (*laughing*). A little shit. I bet he was doing his nut.

MICHAEL. He was. I left him in the woods. Went home for my tea.

CARL (*laughing*). You crack me up. You do.

MICHAEL. Could borrow Mr Singh's Jack Russell. Go to the woods.

CARL. I told you, me and our kid got to look for Leighton Spears. He got himself a shit job an' all. Fucking pen-pusher. Our kid wants to have a word in his ear. Got a suit and one of them, you know, badges on a string and everything.

MICHAEL. Mrs Spears told my mam he's a banker.

CARL. He's not a banker, Mikey, for fuck's sake. He works part time in the Lloyds call-centre off the high street. Selling insurance. Banker my arse. Wanker more like.

MICHAEL. You said we was going to the woods.

*Beat.*

You can bring your brother, Carl.

CARL. Think our kid's gonna wanna hang out with you?

MICHAEL. We could go down the woods, Carl.

CARL. Fucking hell, Mikey. Don't you ever give it a rest? Didn't I tell you I got things to do.

MICHAEL. Did you bring your pellet gun?

CARL. You needs target practice before I let you loose on a pellet gun. You gotta do it right.

MICHAEL. I been practising. Been down the allotments when my mam's not there.

CARL. Bet your mam don't like that. Don't like you messing around with guns.

MICHAEL. She don't know, Carl. Her head would go.

CARL. You tells lies to your mam, do you, Mikey?

MICHAEL. No.

CARL. What she don't know won't hurt her, is that how it is?

MICHAEL. No.

*CARL lights a fag.*

*Pause.*

*Watches* MICHAEL.

CARL. I saw your mam when we first moved yer walking up the high street. And for a minute there I only thought it was my fucking old lady, Mikey. From the back like. Something in her walk. I'm thinking 'What the fuck, what's my old lady doing yer?' When she turned round I could see it weren't her. Did my fucking head in for a second though.

What's your mam's name, Mikey?

MICHAEL. Gloria.

CARL. That's it. Gloria.

Another time I sees her talking to Robbie Coles on the doorstep.

In her dressing gown she was, with a fag.

Laughing an' giving it all that to Robbie Coles.

Half her age, he is.

Then she's calling across the street to Mr Singh.

Just like my mam. That's what I thought.

*Drags his fag.*

My mam fucked off when I was a kid, Mikey boy.

Fed up of the old man battering three kinds of shit out of her, no doubt.

MICHAEL. Are we going to the woods, Carl?

CARL. Your ol' man fucked off. He went cos of her. Cos of Gloria.

MICHAEL. My mam said he just went.

CARL. I could see what she was in five minutes, giving it all that. She been lying to you.

MICHAEL. He just went, that's all.

CARL. You should go an' find him, your old man. He probably been waiting for you to come looking for him.

MICHAEL. He went when I was a kid.

CARL. She fucked it up there for you, mate, cos you should be around some men. It's your right. Men needs men in their packs.

MICHAEL. I hangs around with Mr Singh sometimes. He takes me down the cash-and-carry with my mam.

CARL. Like me, innit. You wants to be like me, don't you, Mikey.

*No response.*

What you up to Saturday?

MICHAEL. Nothing, Carl.

CARL. I'll take you Saturday. To the woods. We'll set some traps.

MICHAEL. We'll go to the woods Saturday. Set some traps. Catch some rats.

CARL. We're after the clean kill, Mikey boy. Don't want any shit. Our kid hangs 'em by their tails all squealing and spitting, shoots the fuckers through the head. Pellets goes straight through. Out the other side. They don't die they just squeals louder. He's a twisted fucker.

MICHAEL. Gotta get the ammo right. That's pointed pellets does that and a fast shooter. Straight through 'em, like that. Twisted fucker.

CARL. You calling our kid twisted?

MICHAEL. Just saying.

CARL. I'll let you away with it. Once. D'you hear that?

MICHAEL. Once. He is a twisted fucker though, Carl.

CARL. Yeah well. You knows it. I knows it.

MICHAEL. The rats knows it.

CARL. Postie knows it too.

MICHAEL. Robbie Coles?

CARL. I'm saying nothing.

MICHAEL. But you just said.

CARL. Shut the fuck up. What the fuck you saying?

MICHAEL. You just said.

CARL. You calling me a grass, you little prick?

MICHAEL. No. I'm not calling you nothing.

CARL. Don't call me a grass, shit-for-brains.

MICHAEL. I'm not, Carl.

CARL. You're the grass.

   CARL *moves off from the wall.*

   D'you hear me?

   *On his mobile. Phone to ear. Walks away.*

   (*To* MICHAEL.) You little prick.

   MICHAEL *grabs his carrier bag and follows him.*

## Scene Four

*Friday, evening.*

GLORIA *and* MICHAEL.

*The allotment.*

*Sat together on two upturned crates, sharing chips from paper.*

*Two new pots waiting to be dug in on the table.*

*A ball bounces.*

GLORIA. You gave him the fiver.

MICHAEL. Yes.

GLORIA. And what did he say?

MICHAEL. Nothing.

GLORIA. And he didn't give you no change?

MICHAEL. He didn't give me no change, Mam.

GLORIA. And he gave you the chips.

MICHAEL. He gave me the chips.

GLORIA. And he took the fiver?

MICHAEL. Yes.

GLORIA. All of it?

MICHAEL. Yes.

GLORIA. So these chips have just cost me a sodding fiver.

MICHAEL. Yes.

GLORIA. You're not lying to me, are you, Michael?

MICHAEL. I'm not lying.

GLORIA. Cos I'll know.

MICHAEL. I'm not lying.

GLORIA. I only got to say something to Lisa and she'll have a word with her fella.

MICHAEL. He's a goon.

GLORIA. I don't want to make a fool of myself going down there accusing someone of stealing my fiver. Even if he is a goon.

MICHAEL. Not lying, Mam.

GLORIA. Cos I gives you all you need, don't I? Makes sure you're fed. Looks after you.

So there'd be no need to take money from me. Michael.

MICHAEL. Not lying, Mam.

GLORIA *takes a swig of beer.*

*Eat chips.*

*Ball bouncing.*

GLORIA. Nobody said nothing about Mrs Spears' cat?

MICHAEL. No.

GLORIA. Cos it'll be all around the estate by now.

MICHAEL. No one said nothing.

GLORIA. Imagine that, Michael. To wake up and find your cat hung up over your door.

MICHAEL. Leighton Spears works part time in the call-centre off the high street.

GLORIA. Mrs Spears thought it was one of her Christmas decorations come loose over the ornamental archway. Told her Leighton to go and sort it out. Well of course...

MICHAEL. He's not a banker, Mam.

GLORIA. It'll be them two. Them brothers. Mrs Spears said as much herself when I saw her this morning. 'It'll be them brothers,' she said. 'It always is,' I said. You make sure you keeps out of their way, Michael. They're always on the look-out for trouble.

I told the police.

MICHAEL. Grassing? Was the police there, Mam?

GLORIA. They was outside Mrs Spears' when I finished my shift, weren't they. I thought I'd go over and tell 'em all about the trouble on the estate that they don't seem to give two shits about. Lisa only left her car up the back lane for half an hour an' it was on bricks by the time she got back. And Mr Singh have had his back window broken twice this week with no attending officer. Low priority is Mr Singh and his window.

MICHAEL. Is he going down the cash-and-carry? I needs some grit.

GLORIA. Mrs Spears was in hell of a state. So I told 'em. I said they could do worse than giving them brothers' house a knock. 'No. 22,' I says, 'You can't miss it, there's a fridge on the front.'

MICHAEL *scrunches up the newspaper and gives it to* GLORIA.

Said they'd have a word. Bugger me if they didn't go straight over. Knocks on the door. Christ. Should've seen him, Michael. The father. Kicking off, he was, in their faces quick as a flash. I thought they'd have him for verbal assault. The language on him. He's a fucking disgrace. I didn't hang around to watch him plume his feathers. I was knackered anyway after my shift. Just wanted to put my feet up.

You can dig them roses in for me after your dinner have settled. Brighten the place up a bit.

GLORIA *picks up the roses.*

MICHAEL. They don't like being moved.

GLORIA. Tell you that, did they.

MICHAEL. Their leaves drop.

*Ball bouncing.*

MICHAEL *gets up and starts digging.*

*A half-dead rose comes off in* GLORIA*'s hand.*

*Looks at half-dead rose.*

*Smells it, picks off a few dead petals. Crushes them in her hand. Smells them again.*

GLORIA. Used to pick all the petals off the roses when I was a kid and try and make perfume out of them. Soaked them in water. Used to use the water out of the lav. Thought that's what they did. With it being called toilet water an' all.

*Smiles.*

*A moment.*

*Looks again at the rose. Puts it behind her ear.*

Look at me, Michael.

*Clicks her heels and positions her hands flamenco-style.*

MICHAEL *digging.*

GLORIA *does it again.*

MICHAEL *digging.*

GLORIA *still in position.*

Michael. Michael. Look at me.

MICHAEL *stops digging.*

GLORIA *does it again.*

MICHAEL. You look like a silly arse.

GLORIA. I wanna be a silly arse, Michael.

MICHAEL *digging.*

Come and dance with me, son.

MICHAEL. No.

GLORIA. Like we used to. Remember. When you was little.
  You used to get on me feet and we'd dance around.

*No response.*

Remember, Michael.

GLORIA *acts out them dancing around.*

*No response.*

GLORIA *stops dancing, disappointed.*

Couldn't do that now though with the size of you.

*Swigs her beer.*

*Pulls the rose from behind her ear and throws it on the floor.*

I been ripped off, I have. I been sold a load of old shite.

MICHAEL. Looks like shit anyways.

*A look at* MICHAEL.

*Ball bounces.*

GLORIA. Stick it up your arse.

MICHAEL. Stick it up *your* arse.

GLORIA. You only gets away with your lip cos there's no man
  yer to pull you in line.

MICHAEL. There's no man yer cos he fucked off away from
  you.

GLORIA. Fucked off away from me, did he?

MICHAEL. Gonna go and find him, my ol' man.

GLORIA. 'Your ol' man'? 'Your ol' man', Michael, is it?

MICHAEL. I should be around some men. Gonna find him, I am.

GLORIA. Gonna find him, are you?

MICHAEL. I am.

GLORIA. Is that what you're gonna do? And how you gonna
  do that?

MICHAEL. Gonna look for him.

GLORIA. Where you gonna look, Michael? Under the toadstool at the bottom of the garden? At the end of the fucking rainbow? Or maybe he's a bit like yourself, Michael, maybe he's away with the fairies somewhere, I think there's a whole group of them living down the Bluebell Woods under Peacock's Ridge, why don't you try asking the leprechaun that lives in the oak tree for directions?

For fuck's sake, Michael.

MICHAEL. Don't care what you says. I'm gonna go and live with him, I reckon.

GLORIA. Are you. Well go on then, son.

Fuck off. Pack your fucking bags and find the cheating selfish bastard.

MICHAEL *doesn't move.*

You wanna be grateful he didn't stick around to drag you up.

MICHAEL. Didn't stick around *you.*

GLORIA. Oh, is that it? Didn't stick around me, is it? You keep telling yourself that, son.

*Pause. Tension for a while.* GLORIA *lights a fag.*

*Drinks her beer.*

*Drags her fag.*

*Watches* MICHAEL.

*Something's not right. Something.*

*Paces.*

*Circles.*

*Drains her beer.*

*Ball bounces.*

Sodding roses.

MICHAEL *back to digging.*

GLORIA *back to acting the dance.*

I could get on your feet, Michael.

MICHAEL. I'm digging.

GLORIA. We could dance.

MICHAEL. Don't want to.

*Sings, jogs the memory. Sings the first couple of lines of Doris Day's 'Que Sera, Sera'.*

I'm digging.

GLORIA. Come here.

MICHAEL *is reluctant.*

Michael.

*Reluctant.*

One dance. Then you can go back to your digging.

*Stops digging.*

Just one. Then you can dig all the way to sodding Australia.

*Reluctantly comes to her.*

*She stands on his feet.*

*Awkward.*

You gotta move your feet, son.

MICHAEL. I'm trying.

GLORIA. Christ, Michael, you gotta move your sodding feet or there's no point in me standing on them.

*Starts moving slowly.*

You gotta move them like we're dancing, son.

MICHAEL. You're hurting me.

GLORIA. Christ, I'm not that heavy.

MICHAEL. Are that heavy.

*Takes off her shoes and gets back on.*

*Starts moving more freely.*

*Less awkward.*

CARL.

*Watching.*

*Still.*

*Unseen.*

GLORIA. I thought of leaving this place.

Maybe go to Spain. Dance the flamenco with a real matador.

*Dancing.*

I used to think I'd like Spain, Michael.

*Dancing.*

*More relaxed.*

Used to think this place was a shithole.

MICHAEL. It is a shithole.

GLORIA. Yes, this place is a first-class shithole, son, but you know what, Michael, the truth of the matter is, the whole world's a bloody shithole.

MICHAEL. The whole world's a bloody shithole.

GLORIA. And that led me to thinking – better the shithole you know.

MICHAEL (*laughing*). Better the shithole you know, Mam.

*Closer.*

*Humming 'Que Sera, Sera'.*

*Hanging on to each other.*

*Still.*

CARL.

*Unseen.*

*Leaves.*

*Pull away from each other.*

*Looks at* MICHAEL.

GLORIA. Michael?

MICHAEL. Yes, Mam.

GLORIA. Give me my change, son.

## Scene Five

*Saturday, afternoon.*

*The woods.*

CARL *and* MICHAEL. CARL *is holding the materials for snare traps as he talks.*

CARL. And I got my old man giving it all that to the cops –
'You fucking coming knocking on my door about a shitty-
arsed cat,' telling them all about his rights and harassment
and all that shit.

And our kid's on a right downer, he's not shifted his arse all
morning and I'm thinking I fucking knows where this is
going, don't I. My old man's gonna shut the door to Jack and
Jill and wanna take it out on someone. Been treating me like
a fucking errand boy all morning.

MICHAEL. You gonna show me the snare?

CARL (*mimics*). 'Get me my fucking cider, lad. Twenty
Lambert & Butlers, our kid.'

They'll be getting me one of them uniforms for the shop I'm
down there so much.

MICHAEL. Lisa's shop.

CARL. Get him his cider, put on his bet, fix him up with some hardcore and we can sleep soundly, if you knows what I means.

MICHAEL. We was going to do snare traps.

CARL. You don't give it up, d'you?

*Talks as he starts to set the trap.*

Our kid's been looking at getting himself a fuck-off foothold trap. Knows this guy, into all this weird shit.

MICHAEL. For the rats.

CARL. It's like a big fuck-off metal jaw. Catch all sorts. Reckons he can catch foxes and badgers with it.

MICHAEL. You have to be careful with them traps though, Carl. They catches people's dogs and cats.

*CARL stops setting.*

CARL. You thinks I catch people's dogs and cats?

*Looks at* MICHAEL.

MICHAEL. You have to be careful with them traps, though.

*CARL back to trap.*

CARL. It has its problems, Mikey boy. That's why I prefers the snare. Come yer I'll show you.

*Patiently shows* MICHAEL *how to set traps.*

You got it, Mikey boy. I can learn you loads of shit out yer in the woods.

MICHAEL. The oldest trapping method is the deadfall.

CARL. You're all that, Mikey boy – (*Mimes 'talk' with hand.*) You tells me all about shit but you can't do it, can you? You needs someone like me to show you how it all works, don't you?

You're like one of them books, Mikey boy, them big ones.

MICHAEL. Encyclopedias.

CARL. That's 'em.

MICHAEL. Foothold traps are seen as cruel by animal-welfare
groups.

CARL. That's cos the fuckers chew off their own limbs to get
out of 'em. Daft sods. Our kid don't give a shit. Said if he's
left with a leg he'll put a cord through it, Wear it like a
necklace. Like a trophy, you know.

MICHAEL. Or a keyring.

CARL. He don't want to look like a fucking poof, Mikey, with
a fucking furry keyring.

*They finish setting the trap.*

CARL *starts to roll a fag.*

*Watches* MICHAEL.

And talking of looking like a fucking poof, Mikey boy. You
needs to sort your threads. Look at you. You wants to stop
letting your mam buy your gear.

MICHAEL *looks down at his clothes.*

You wants to get some threads like what I got.

Like me and our kid.

MICHAEL. I wants to get some new threads, Carl.

CARL. Make sure they fits you right as well. Looking like a
nonce ain't the fucking way forward. I bet you gets all sorts of
shit thrown your way looking like a nonce, don't you, Mikey.

MICHAEL *says nothing.*

CARL *notices.*

You had trouble before, have you, Mikey?

MICHAEL *says nothing.*

You can't tell me nothing I don't already know. Bet you've
had fucking trouble all your life, you.

CARL *watches* MICHAEL.

That's all gonna change. I won't let no fucker near you.

*Back to traps.*

See, like that. What did I tell you. You got it.

*Pats him on the back.*

I can teach you a load of shit no other fucker's gonna bother with. And in the end that's how you wins. You're gonna know stuff that no one else will.

The element of surprise, it's called.

*Looks at* MICHAEL.

MICHAEL *pleased with himself.*

CARL *carries on with traps.*

MICHAEL *watches how* CARL *moves. Looks at* CARL*'s clothes,* CARL*'s hair.*

*Mimics him in some way. Not comical.*

MICHAEL. I'll go up the high street. They got some gear up the high street. I'll go to that one by the Labour Club.

CARL. You knows the Labour Club, don't you, Mikey? It's your mam's favourite place, ain't it? She likes a drink, your mam.

MICHAEL. She likes a drink, Carl. Likes to have fun.

CARL. I seen her coming home from the club loads of times, different men an' all. She's hanging around that Darren, ain't she?

MICHAEL. Don't know, Carl.

CARL. She's off her face, her. Bet you has your hands full with her, don't you, Mikey boy.

MICHAEL. I do have my hands full with her, Carl.

CARL. Bet she went off her head when you told her you was hanging around with me.

MICHAEL. Didn't tell her that, Carl. She'd go off her head.

*Pause.*

CARL. Families, Mikey. Can't live with 'em, can't live without 'em. A right pain in the arse they are.

MICHAEL. Can't live without them, Carl.

CARL. Talking of which, I got to get our kid some pain relief. Get a bit for me and my old man while I'm at it. Keep him sweet.

MICHAEL. Go to Blake's on the high street?

CARL. Are you a doctor now, are you?

MICHAEL. Blake's Chemist. Opens nine to six Monday to Saturday except for Wednesday's half-day.

CARL. What the fuck?

MICHAEL. It closes at one.

CARL. How about Herbie the Herb? What are his opening hours, Mikey?

MICHAEL. Don't know.

CARL. You fucking crack me up, you do. Tell you what I'd like to see. I'd like to see you off your head. That'd be a fucking scream. How 'bout it, Mikey? Shall we get off our fucking heads?

MICHAEL (*joining in laughing*). Yeah, I'd like to see that.

CARL. We'll pay Herbie a visit. He'll sort us out. Get us some Alaskan Thunder Fuck. We'll come up the woods.

MICHAEL. That'd be a scream.

CARL. We might see Lisa and that prick she's fucking from the chippy.

MICHAEL. She's not fucking no one.

CARL. You'd like that, Mikey, wouldn't you? Watching Lisa giving it all that – (*Mimes Lisa giving a blowjob.*)

CARL *pissing himself.*

*Not funny.*

MICHAEL. No.

CARL *watches* MICHAEL.

CARL (*puts the fag behind his ear*). We'll come when it's dark.

MICHAEL. I don't come out when it's dark, Carl.

CARL. What the fuck. Melt, do you?

MICHAEL. I go home for my tea. I don't go out after tea.

CARL. How old are you? For fuck's sake. You got hair on your bollocks, haven't you?

MICHAEL. Yes.

CARL. We'll camp out all night.

MICHAEL. I sleep in my bed. In my house.

CARL. Who needs a bed, Mikey. I camps out yer in the woods all the time when I needs to get away from the old man.

I was in the Scouts, weren't I.

*No response.*

Went camping with them and all that.

Fucking best days of my life.

MICHAEL. My mam wants me home before it's dark.

CARL. Was you in the Scouts when you was a kid, Mikey?

MICHAEL. No, but I knows about it. Akela the leader.

CARL. 'The Cub Scout follows Akela.'

MICHAEL. 'Because of his age and his cunning,
  because of his gripe and his paw,
  In all that the Law leaveth open,
  the word of your Head Wolf is Law.'

CARL *joins in. For the fun. For a moment a kid. Having a laugh.*

BOTH. 'Now these are the Laws of the Jungle,
      and many and mighty are they;
      But the head and the hoof of the Law
      and the haunch and the hump is – Obey!'

CARL. Got trees and bushes and leaves and shit. That's all you
      needs. I got a badge for building a fire. Some outdoor badge.

      I'll make us a camp.

MICHAEL. I'm not camping, Carl. I go home. Have my tea.
      Watch the telly. Go to bed. My mam don't want me out in
      the dark.

      *Back to reality.*

CARL. What the fuck you doing?

MICHAEL. Not doing nothing.

CARL. You trying to teach me now, Mikey, is that what you
      thinks you're doing?

MICHAEL. No. Just saying.

CARL. Don't. Cos it makes me look like a prick and you don't
      wanna make me look like a prick after all I done for you.
      Cos I'm your leader, Mikey, I'm your Akela. That's how it's
      gonna work for us, ain't it.

      *Takes fag from behind his ear.*

MICHAEL. Sorry, Carl.

CARL. Fucking will be sorry. You hear me.

      *Lights fag.*

MICHAEL. My mam…

CARL (*stops him talking about his mam*). I only got men
      around me, ain't I. No pussy bitches giving me all that. My
      old man when he's off on one. That's real men, Mikey.
      That's what I'm talking about.

      *Plays with wire for traps.*

      *Swings wire.*

*Drags his fag slowly.*

It's all about the team for this lot. Like with me and our kid. All for one.

MICHAEL. Are you and our kid a team, Carl?

CARL. It's not good for boys our age to have nothing to do. Gets up to all sorts then, don't we.

*Beat.*

We had this dog when we was kids. Scruffy little bastard it was. It had pups.

My mam loved that dog.

We didn't get that, me and our kid. How she could leave that dog.

My ol' man knew she loved that dog.

He hung them in the yard. Made me tie the knots.

Went at them with a rake.

Left them hanging there like some sort of decoration.

*Plays with wire.*

That's the thing, see. I works in a team. It's what I'm used to. And I was thinking about you and me. And I was thinking about you being in my team now.

MICHAEL. I wanna be in your team, Carl. You and our kid.

CARL. Didn't I tell you to keep away from him, Mikey? Didn't I say he's a twisted fucker? Is that not what I said?

MICHAEL. I thought you wanted me in your team, Carl.

CARL. My team. You and me.

MICHAEL. You and me.

CARL. Have you heard of 'Blood In', Mikey?

MICHAEL. No.

CARL. If you wants to be part of my team then I expects you to show me you're loyal to me. That's what 'Blood In' means.

MICHAEL. I wants to be part of your team.

CARL. I been thinking about him from the chippy. Him with the hat.

I'm telling you, Mikey, this fucker makes himself look like an arsehole with his 'Yes, indeedy' an' all that but he's not all fucking there.

MICHAEL. I never seen him without his hat, Carl. My mam thinks he got bad hair.

CARL. He needs teaching a fucking lesson cos now I'm coming to think about it. I don't fucking like the way he looks at me. You know he short-changed our kid a couple of weeks back an' all. He needs a lesson all right. That little rat he calls a dog. That little rat been shitting on my front garden.

MICHAEL. He's a goon.

CARL. And he's fucking your missus, Mikey. Your Lisa. I bet he don't leave her alone. I bet he's after her day and night. You gonna let him get away with that.

MICHAEL. He's not fucking Lisa.

CARL. Not after we finished with him.

MICHAEL. What you gonna do, Carl?

*Pause.*

CARL. What are *you* gonna do, Mikey?

*Pause.*

*Flicks wire at* MICHAEL.

CARL *laughs.*

MICHAEL *rubs his arm, hurt.*

CARL *whips* MICHAEL, *harder this time, laughing.*

*Hurt.*

CARL *stops laughing.*

I asked you a question.

What are you gonna do?

MICHAEL. I don't want no trouble, Carl.

CARL. Thing is. What you needs to know about the 'Blood In'
    is that blood needs to be shed. That's the point. But thing is,
    whose blood is shed is up to you, Mikey.

*Pause.*

His or yours, Mikey boy.

## Scene Six

*Early hours of Sunday morning (one a.m.).*

*The still of the night.*

GLORIA *worse for wear.*

*A football is being bounced. We hear the noise of the bounce
before we see what it is.*

CARL *appears, holding the football in one hand, a bag of chips
in the other.*

*He sees* GLORIA.

*Approaches her. Circles her.*

*Stands next to her. Opens his chips. Starts eating.*

*Says nothing. Watches* GLORIA.

*Offers her a chip.*

*No.*

CARL *stands next to* GLORIA *like soldiers on parade.*

GLORIA *watches his every move.*

*He smiles.*

*Again offers her a chip.*

*She thinks about it.*

*Go on then.*

*They share chips.*

*He copies every movement – hand to mouth. Hand to mouth. Chews. Chews.*

*She laughs – silly sod.*

*He scrumples the chip paper.*

*Drops it to the floor.*

CARL *smiles.*

GLORIA *smiles back.*

*He holds her eye.*

*Longer than he should.*

CARL *smiles.*

GLORIA *goes to her bag for a fag.*

*Struggles to find a light.*

CARL *lights her fag.*

*He bows dramatically, chivalry, offers her the lighter.*

*She smiles.*

*Takes the lighter.*

*Drags her fag.*

*Again he bows dramatically.*

GLORIA *laughs – silly sod.*

CARL *clicks his heels, flamenco-style.*

*Adopts a matador stance.*

GLORIA *laughs.*

*Intrigued.*

CARL *takes off his hoodie and swishes it, matador-style.*
*Finishes by tying it around his neck as a cape.*

*Strikes a matador pose.*

GLORIA *laughs.*

*Again he bows.*

*Holds out his hands – would you like this dance?*

GLORIA *smiles.*

*Holds his eye.*

*Longer than she should.*

*Outs her fag.*

*Takes his hand.*

*Eye to eye.*

*They dance.*

*Eye to eye.*

*Closer now.*

*She holds him.*

*Tender.*

*Touches his face.*

*Stop.*

*Drops her hands.*

*Pulls away.*

*He circles her.*

*Stands behind her.*

*Puts his arms around her.*

*Holds on to her.*

*She responds.*

*He pushes her away – as if.*

*Angry and confused.*

*Confused and pissed.*

*Grabs the chips. Throws them at him.*

*Starts to walk off.*

*Stumbles a bit. Pissed.*

*Throws the chips back at her.*

GLORIA *looks at the chips. Looks at* CARL *– how fucking dare he? Goes for him.*

*Pushes her away – pisshead.*

*Circles her.*

*Intimidated.*

GLORIA *swings for him.*

CARL *grabs her hand before she makes contact.*

*Holds her wrist tightly.*

*Tighter.*

GLORIA *struggles to get free. Furious. Can't break out of his grip.*

*They look at each other, face to face, eye to eye.*

*Circle, still holding each other.*

*He looks at her.*

*Up and down. Intensely. Takes her in.*

*She watches him.*

*Lost and pissed.*

*Breathes him in.*

*Closes her eyes.*

*Feels him.*

*Feels his body.*

*Starts to put her hand into his trousers.*

*He pushes her away.*

*Looks at her.*

*A moment.*

*Disgusted – filthy whore.*

*Throws her to the floor amongst the chips.*

*Throws chips at her.*

*Looks at her. Disgusted.*

*Picks up his ball. Bounces.*

*Looks at her.*

*On the floor.*

*Walks off, bouncing his ball.*

## Scene Seven

*Sunday, afternoon.*

*The allotment.*

MICHAEL *digging in the new roses.*

GLORIA *distracted. Not drinking.*

CARL *watching.*

MICHAEL. Got me any grit yet?

    *No response.*

    I need grit.

GLORIA. I'm not talking to you about the shit bleedin' grit.

MICHAEL. Or heavy-grain sand.

*No response.*

Just a couple of bags would do it.

*No response.*

I needs a couple of bags.

*No response.*

I'll get some.

GLORIA. Oh yeah.

MICHAEL. Get it myself.

GLORIA. That's right.

MICHAEL. Get some from Wilson's on the high street.

GLORIA. You do that.

MICHAEL. Two bags.

GLORIA. How you gonna get two bags of grit home?

MICHAEL. I'll get it home.

GLORIA. Gonna carry it on your back all that way, are you?

MICHAEL. I'll get some.

GLORIA. Two bags. On your back.

MICHAEL. Get it from Wilson's, that's what I'll do.

GLORIA. Like a donkey.

MICHAEL. One bag of grit, one bag of heavy-grain sand.

GLORIA. I'll get you a straw hat, Michael. I'll get you a straw hat like one of them donkeys on the beach.

MICHAEL. It's all about the grain size and the grading.

GLORIA. Shut up, Michael.

MICHAEL. Not soft sand. We don't want soft sand. A uniform sand is no good for our purpose.

GLORIA. I've had a guts-full. A bloody guts-full.

MICHAEL. There's more confusion regarding sand than any
other of the aggregates. It's all to do with the grading.

GLORIA. Shut up, just shut up, will you.

MICHAEL. You got to get the right grain size.

GLORIA. Shut up about the fucking grit.

*Pause.*

MICHAEL *aware of* GLORIA'*s mood.*

*Back to digging.*

*Silence.*

*As long as is comfortable.*

Something happened last night, Michael. Across the way. In
that house. No. 22. Looked like all hell broke loose. Woke
me up. Shouting and screaming, things smashing an' that.
There was an ambulance. And police in and out.

God only knows what happened.

*Nothing.*

What you got to say about it, Michael?

MICHAEL. About what?

GLORIA. 'Bout what happened last night. Across the way there.

MICHAEL. Nothing. Got nothing to say.

GLORIA. No?

MICHAEL. No.

GLORIA. Cos that's funny that. I was thinking you'd have an
opinion on what happened over there.

MICHAEL. Haven't got no opinion on nothing.

GLORIA. Thought you'd have maybe known something about
it. Or showed some concern. Something like that.

MICHAEL. Don't know nothing.

GLORIA. Did you hear about him from the chippy's dog, Michael? Did you hear what happened to his dog?

MICHAEL. Don't know nothing.

GLORIA. They reckon it's lucky to be alive. He'd been tied up in the woods, Michael, and he'd had all his fur cut off him and shit rubbed all over him. And he was left like that. Left for dead, Lisa said.

MICHAEL. I told you. I don't know nothing about nothing.

GLORIA. You know, Michael, I been thinking that you haven't been yourself lately. That something's not been right with you.

MICHAEL. Am myself. Who else I'm gonna be anyway?

GLORIA. An' then I was thinking how things have changed since them lads moved onto the estate. Not like it used to be, you know.

The earth rumbled when they arrived, Michael.

The soil shifted.

MICHAEL. What you talking about? Talking bollocks, Mam.

GLORIA. You're hanging around with them brothers, Michael.

MICHAEL. No.

GLORIA. You are, Michael.

MICHAEL. No.

GLORIA. You're lying to me, son.

MICHAEL. Not lying.

GLORIA. You been hanging around them, Michael. I can feel it crawling through my skin, turning my gut.

MICHAEL. Not hanging round them brothers. Just Carl. Just Carl, not our kid.

GLORIA. You can't be around him.

MICHAEL. He's my friend.

GLORIA. Was that who you was with at the chippy?

MICHAEL. Don't know.

GLORIA. You do know, Michael. Lisa told me. Said you was mouthing off. Trying to start trouble. Is that who you are now, is it? Some mouthy little shit who goes round trying to start trouble with people who done you no harm.

MICHAEL. No.

GLORIA. Them boys are behind all the trouble on the estate. Mr Singh caught the one with the eye pissing in his plants just Friday gone.

MICHAEL. Pissing in his pants, pissing in his pants.

GLORIA. You think this is funny, do you?

MICHAEL. Yes.

GLORIA. Is it funny, Michael, is it?

MICHAEL. Yes.

GLORIA. It's not funny, Michael.

MICHAEL. Do what I like, anyways.

GLORIA. You will not.

MICHAEL. Old enough to do what I like. You can't tell me nothing. Do what I like.

GLORIA. You will not. Do you hear me.

MICHAEL. I will.

GLORIA. Will I tell Mr Singh you're going to do what you like from now on, Michael.

MICHAEL. No.

GLORIA. D'you think Mr Singh will think it's funny that you're hanging round the estate up to all sorts with them little shits.

MICHAEL. Not little shits.

GLORIA. No, you're right there, Michael. Cos Mr Singh calls them disgusting little shits. Cos he saw the mess they'd left up Old Mrs Williams' walls after they broke in for the third time. So I'll give you that one, Michael.

MICHAEL. Talking shit, Mam.

GLORIA. Not talking shit, Michael.

MICHAEL. Talking shit again, Mam.

GLORIA. Haven't I told you? Carl, was it? The youngest one?
You stay away from him, you hear me.

MICHAEL. You can't tell me. We're a team, me and Carl. I'm
in his pack now.

GLORIA. No. No more.

MICHAEL. He's not like what you says.

GLORIA. He's sick in the head, Michael. You listen to me. He's
trouble and you stay away. He hurts things. He'll hurt you.
It's what he is.

It don't take a genius to work out who hung Mrs Spears' cat.
And the dog?

That's not you, Michael.

Is that what you wants to be part of?

You wants to be part of that pack?

MICHAEL (*new aggression*). You gotta stop telling me what to
do. You gotta stop buying my threads. Could see what you
are in five minutes. Stood there giving it all that. You don't
tell me what to do. Don't want no pussy bitch telling me
what to do.

GLORIA *slaps him.*

MICHAEL *slaps her back.*

*Shock.*

MICHAEL *shocked.*

*Immediately repentant.*

*Goes to her.*

*Holds on to her.*

GLORIA *unresponsive*.

*Pause.*

GLORIA. You don't go near him again, Michael, or so help me.

MICHAEL. I won't go near him again, Mam.

GLORIA. You promise me.

MICHAEL. I promise, Mam.

GLORIA *and* MICHAEL *hold a look*.

GLORIA *touches his arm, picks up his spade, hands it to him*.

MICHAEL *holds on to his spade*.

Don't tell Mr Singh, Mam.

*Picks up the roses.*

I'll get these flowers in for you.

GLORIA *looks to the sky, looks at the spade, at* MICHAEL. *She knows what's coming.*

GLORIA. You do that, son. Before it rains.

*Lights down to spot on* MICHAEL *digging*.

*A ball bounces.*

MICHAEL *digs*.

*Becomes aware of the bounce.*

*Looks around.*

*Nobody there.*

MICHAEL *digs*.

*Ball bounces.*

*Looks around again.*

*Nothing.*

MICHAEL *digs*.

*Ball bounces to darkness.*

**Scene Eight**

*Sunday, early evening.*

MICHAEL *walking with a bag of shopping through the woods.*

MICHAEL *sees* CARL.

*Cautious.*

MICHAEL. I didn't see you there, Carl.

   *Nothing.*

   All right, Carl. Been to get my mam some fags.

   *Nothing.*

   What's happened, Carl?

   *Nothing.*

   You looks like shit.

CARL. I been in the woods.

   Been here all night as it goes.

MICHAEL. My mam said there was an ambulance at yours last
   night.

   *Picks up* MICHAEL*'s carrier bag of food.*

   Got a pasty. And a Curly Wurly. And my mam's fags.

   CARL *takes the carrier.*

   *Rummages through it.*

   And some Vimto.

   *Takes out pasty. Starts to eat it.*

   *Gulps down Vimto.*

   I got Vimto.

CARL. What the fuck, Mikey. I'm drinking the fucking Vimto
so I knows you got it, don't I?

MICHAEL. Are you hungry, Carl?

CARL. What d'you think. I been yer all night, haven't I? An'
I'll be yer tonight an' all. And tomorrow and the day after
that. I ran, didn't I?

The woods is my fucking home now, Mikey.

MICHAEL. But you can't live here, Carl.

CARL. They found this kid in Russia a few years back. Been
brought up in the wild by wolves all his life. He was barking
and growling and all that shit. And they found him and took
him into this home, thinking that's gonna sort him out an'
that and next thing they know the little fucker's escaped back
to the wild. He's thought 'Fuck this for a laugh I'm back to
my pack where I knows what's what.' He's still out there.
They haven't caught him.

MICHAEL. Is he back with his pack?

CARL. How the fuck do I know? Nobody knows, d'they. He's
in the wild in'e. They haven't been able to catch the slippery
bastard.

MICHAEL *takes one of the sweets.*

MICHAEL. Could be dead.

CARL. He's not dead.

MICHAEL. Could be dead.

CARL. He's not fucking dead.

*Silence.*

MICHAEL *takes a sweet.*

MICHAEL. What happened, Carl?

CARL. He's still out there.

MICHAEL. Your dad'll wonder where you are.

CARL. They'll never get him.

MICHAEL. What about our kid, Carl?

CARL. It's all clearer, see. Out here in the wild. They all knows what's what, the wolves in their packs. They got rules and they obeys. It's clear, then everyone knows what to do.

MICHAEL. What about your pack, Carl? Our kid? Your dad?

CARL. He's not my fucking pack, Mikey. I thought he was an' he ain't. He's seen to that. He's worse than a fucking animal. He's a beast. A fucking monster.

That kid in Russia's a lucky bastard. He got away.

MICHAEL. He could be dead, Carl.

CARL (*snaps*). Our kid's not dead, Mikey.

Cos if that fucking monster... if that's all that's left for me. See that tree there. I'd rather hang myself from that tree than go back to that house. With him.

MICHAEL *looks away. Looks around. Some time.*

MICHAEL. You can tell how old a tree is by its trunk.

You gotta look at the rings. Gotta count the rings.

The oldest tree in the world is nine thousand, five hundred and fifty years old.

CARL. What the fuck you talking about?

*Another sweet. One for each hand.*

MICHAEL. Talking about that tree, Carl.

CARL. I can tell you how old that tree is over there. Without doing any of that shit. I just gotta look at it.

*Takes a moment looking at the tree.*

Really fucking old is how old it is.

MICHAEL. The oak is a common symbol of strength and is the national tree of many countries. Also known as the tree of doors, believed to be gateways between worlds.

CARL. How d'you know shit like that?

MICHAEL *says nothing*.

You says shit like that and then the next minute you're a thick fuck, all dribbling and shit.

*Pause*.

I think that's the biggest fucking tree in the whole woods.

Bet you could see all over the estate if you got to the top of it.

MICHAEL. You could yes.

CARL. Does the leaves come off in the winter?

MICHAEL. Yes. But it don't always look like they do. They turns brown. Clings on. Like they don't wanna drop.

CARL. People hugs trees. I heard that.

*Pause*.

Why do they do that?

*Looks to* MICHAEL *for an answer.*

MICHAEL. Don't know, Carl.

CARL. Does your mam hug you, Mikey?

MICHAEL. Yes.

CARL. I been thinking. About it. About you. About Gloria. I been thinking about if I was her son. About if I was you. Been thinking about what I would be then. Wouldn't be here, would I.

Why does she hug you, Mikey?

MICHAEL. To keep me close, that's what she says. She smells me. I don't know why, Carl. She sniffs my hair.

*Pause*.

CARL *snatches away the sweets*.

CARL *crumbling*.

CARL. I can't get the fucking blood off, it's over my hands and my gear and I can't get it off. Our kid, he's sat there and I'm trying to hold his face together and there's fucking blood everywhere, man. And my old man just keeps at him. And I'm telling him to fucking leave him alone.

It'll be me next time.

And he'll come at me worse just to teach me. He's gone at him with this blade, see, sliced his face. And I can see his teeth, through his cheek. And I'm trying to hold his face.

I'm holding our kid's face together and in my head I'm thinking about the wolves. About the wolves and the Russian. About how they looks after each other. Looks out for each other.

An' I looks at my ol' man an' he won't call for the fucking ambulance in case he gets himself banged up again. He's calling us pussy shits an' kicking off. His cub is fucking bleeding half his face off an' he won't do fuck all.

I'm looking at this blood. On my hands. Sinking in my skin. An' in this blood I'm seeing our kid an' I'm seeing my ol' man. An' I'm seeing me. I'm in there too, Mikey. An' then I'm seeing that it's in me, that blood. That it's running through me an' there's no escaping it, Mikey. I can see it. There's no fucking escaping it cos it's through my veins an' it's beating through my heart an' it's him.

He's in me.

Whatever I do, Mikey.

*Some time.*

MICHAEL *takes a sweet, takes another one and offers it to* CARL.

*Puts his arm around* CARL*'s back.*

I got nowhere to go, Mikey. An' if anything's happened to our kid. I don't know, Mikey. I don't know what happened. Is he dead, Mikey? I ran.

I got no one.

'Cept you.

I can trust you, can't I, Mikey?

*No response.*

Cos if I'm gonna make it out here I gotta be able to trust you.

MICHAEL. I can't see you no more, Carl.

CARL. I got no one.

MICHAEL. My mam don't want no trouble.

*Some time.*

CARL *gets up.*

*Paces.*

*Circles him.*

MICHAEL *doesn't move.*

CARL*'s anger builds, disgusted by his own vulnerability and the let-down.*

CARL. See now we got ourselves a very complicated situation, Mikey boy.

Cos see I trusted you.

I trusted you, you fucking retard.

I fucking trusted you.

MICHAEL *gets up.*

MICHAEL. I gotta go, Carl.

CARL *(mimics).* 'I gotta go, Carl.' Got things to do, have you?

Digging with your fucking spade. Sat with your mam like a fucking poof. Talking about how fucking shit my family is? Is that what you got to do?

MICHAEL. Sorry, Carl.

CARL. Fucking will be sorry. You hear me. You fucking will be sorry.

CARL *pacing, circling*.

Know about lone wolves, Mikey boy?

*No response.*

Course you do. See I always thought that wolves went around in packs. And they do, Mikey. But there's always exceptions, ain't there. Your lone wolf is the exception, Mikey, cos when it chooses to live away from its pack it knows the chances of survival aren't great, so to speak. So it knows it has to be one of two things, Mikey. It either has to be strong as fuck or a nasty little shit. And then it knows it's got a chance. So your strong-as-fuck lone wolf, he finds himself another pack, fights all the fuckers who fancy their chances against him and takes over as leader. The nasty-little-shit lone wolf. Well now he's a different story. Cos he knows he ain't strong enough to get in with a new pack so he gotta live his life using his cunning. He gotta steal and he gotta lie and he gotta take what he can when he can.

But he'll be okay. Because you know what he's doing, Mikey boy?

*No response.*

He's doing whatever the fuck he wants, that's what he's doing. He don't give a shit for no one. He's living for the moment, Mikey.

*No response.*

Seize the day.

MICHAEL. Seize the day, Carl.

CARL. What do you fucking know about it?

MICHAEL. Nothing.

*Back to bouncing.*

CARL. Heard of jousting, Mikey?

MICHAEL. Jousting?

CARL. Course you fucking haven't.

MICHAEL. I heard of jousting.

CARL. Martial contest is jousting. Knights and lances and shit.

MICHAEL. Big horses.

CARL. Big fuck-off horses. Like tanks. Coming at you.

MICHAEL. Like tanks.

CARL. Lances and swords and battleaxes.

MICHAEL. And daggers, Carl. Jousting tournaments uses a load of weapons.

*As he talks,* CARL *picks up a stick.*

CARL. I fucking know that. Loads of weapons.

And masks and shit.

En garde.

CARL *holds the stick like a sword.*

Come on, Mikey. Let's do it. Let's joust, Mikey.

MICHAEL. Don't want to, Carl.

CARL *is circling* MICHAEL, *throws the stick at him.*
MICHAEL *picks it up.*

CARL *picks up another stick. Circles* MICHAEL.

We haven't got horses or nothing.

CARL *runs for* MICHAEL, *almost jabs him in the stomach.*
MICHAEL *moves away. Walking backwards as* CARL
*comes for him again.* MICHAEL *blocks with his stick.*

CARL *laughs.*

MICHAEL *laughs. Unsure.*

CARL *runs at* MICHAEL. *They tumble around childlike,
using the sticks. The jabs from* CARL *get more menacing.*

*He whacks* MICHAEL *full-force, taking the wind out of him.*
MICHAEL *falls to the floor.* CARL *is unaffected by*
MICHAEL*'s pain. Time passes as* MICHAEL *gets himself*
*together.*

CARL. Animals do jousting, Mikey.

MICHAEL. Do they, Carl?

CARL. I saw it on one of my ol' man's films.

MICHAEL. I never heard of that, Carl.

CARL. Ducks and these worms. Flatworms or some shit.

MICHAEL. I don't know about that, Carl.

CARL. With their cocks.

*Silence.*

And fucking benders do it. Fucking dirty poofs. They
fucking love it.

MICHAEL. I want to go home, Carl.

CARL. What the fuck did you say?

MICHAEL. Don't know.

CARL *slaps him around the head.*

CARL. Fucking dumb-arse. You shut the fuck up. Cos what you
gotta know is, what you got to understand is that I'm a lone
wolf now, Michael.

I gotta look out for myself now.

An' I'm not having you coming here pissing on my land.

I ain't letting you get away with it.

You're in my lair and you'll do as I say.

MICHAEL. Please, Carl.

CARL. Did I say you could speak?

*Hits him around the head again.*

MICHAEL. Please.

CARL. Keep your fucking mouth shut or you'll have my fist through it.

MICHAEL *starts crying*.

Are you fucking crying, you pussy shit.

CARL *holds a crying* MICHAEL.

Now these are the Laws of the Jungle,
and many and mighty are they;
But the head and the hoof of the Law
and the haunch and the hump is – Obey!'

CARL *holds* MICHAEL'*s face, wipes his tears. Menacing, intimidating*.

*Looks at* MICHAEL'*s face*.

*Kisses* MICHAEL *forcefully*.

MICHAEL *tries to fight him off*. CARL *pushes* MICHAEL, *slaps him. Hits him*.

MICHAEL *tries to break free*.

CARL *overpowers him*.

*The submissive wolf*.

MICHAEL *in a heap, curled in a ball*.

CARL *kicks him. Beats him*.

CARL *undoes his flies and pisses over him*.

## Scene Nine

*Darkness*

*Sunday, night.*

*The still of the night.*

*The allotment.*

*Deserted.*

MICHAEL.

*Dishevelled. Dirty. Disorientated.*

*Digging.*

*Hysteria.*

*Calming himself.*

*Digging.*

*Confused.*

*Abused.*

*Digging.*

GLORIA.

*Her son.*

*Beaten.*

*Bewildered.*

*He digs.*

*She goes to him.*

*Holds his face.*

*Looks at him.*

*Blood.*

*His torn clothes.*

*He digs.*

*She holds him.*

*He digs.*

*She holds him.*

*Hums.*

*He stops.*

*She holds him.*

*Time passes.*

*Listen.*

*Time passes.*

*She holds him.*

GLORIA *stands.*

*Picks up* MICHAEL*'s spade.*

**Scene Ten**

*The woods.*

CARL.

*The oak tree.*

*Pacing.*

*Around and around the tree.*

GLORIA.

CARL *on the tree, climbs to the top.*

*There's a hysteria to his manner, at times more heightened than others.*

CARL. I was right. I can see. All over. I can see it all. More than the estate. I can see the whole bloody world.

*Beat.*

People say they wants to travel the world. They say that, don't they. 'I want to travel the world,' see all the sights. They says they wants to go to the Great Wall of China and they wants to go to India to sit in front of the Taj Mahal or go to the Amazon Rainforest and shit like that. That's what they says, don't they. Niagara Falls and all that.

*Beat.*

It's all there but I can't see it. I can't see any of it.

*She swings at the tree with the spade.*

*Again she swings.*

*Again and again.*

*She drops to her knees at the base of the tree.*

*Time passes.*

GLORIA. You know, I wanted a girl. Had it all planned. I was gonna call her Caron. With an O. Didn't want a boy.

When I had him I thought they'd given me the wrong baby.

He wouldn't feed or do nothing right.

Kept being sick.

An' I'd look at him an' I'd think 'Who the bloody hell are you? Who are you to come into my life and take it all away?' And he'd look at me with them big eyes. And in here would ache.

And I'd wash him and put his little outfit on him, wrap him up warm and put him in the pram and we'd come down the allotment and he'd lie there and smile and this feeling in here wouldn't go away. And I knew I'd do anything for him and I wouldn't change him for the world.

CARL. *Holding a rope. Speaks as he attaches it to the tree.*

CARL. Slip knots, half hitch, reef knots. Left over right, right over left. I knows that. It's all in here – (*Points to head.*) Funny that, ain't it. How it's all in there.

For ever.

Never goes away.

*Adjusts the length of the rope.*

Did a badge for knots. When I was in the Scouts.

Did some badges an' all that shit. Wanted to be a fireman. So they tells me 'Do the badge with the knots.' They says 'It'll come in handy when you're older.'

(*Laughs.*) They was fucking right there.

*Looks at noose.*

People hugs trees.

I tried it. Tried to hear it breathe.

But at the end of the day, it's just a fucking tree, ain't it?

GLORIA. In some cultures, the mams won't look after their babies if they finds out there's something wrong with them. I heard that. Pagans I think. Something like that. Animals do the same.

They takes the runts off, don't they?

Leaves them to die.

Your mother.

She should have put her runt out to the woods.

Left him to die.

CARL (*looks to* GLORIA). She did.

*Pause.*

GLORIA. You have to go. You see that, don't you. You have to.

Because what you did to my son. There's no coming back from that.

CARL. I got nowhere. I got no one.

GLORIA. You wants me to feel sorry for you. Me, feel sorry for you.

What you done to my son and you thinks I'll be sorry for you.

D'you think I'll cry for you cos your mother left you when you was a baby?

Cos you've had a hard life?

CARL. Shut up. You just shut the fuck up. You don't know nothing about it. You don't know nothing about my mother, you don't know nothing about none of it.

GLORIA. Are you crying? Are you crying now?

CARL. Not fucking crying. I'm the lone wolf. The lone wolf now.

GLORIA. Running away and hiding. Whimpering. You're no wolf.

You're a runt. A weak little runt.

CARL. No. You shut up. You shut your mouth.

GLORIA. You're a coward. Sat there crying with your rope. Waking the woods with your bay. It's all words. Pathetic coward words.

CARL. Don't you fucking say I'm a coward. Don't you fucking dare.

GLORIA. You haven't got the courage to do it.

It takes a strong wolf to do that. To take responsibilty for what they done.

A leader.

You haven't got it in you.

You ran from your pack when they needed you most.

You're a coward.

CARL. Don't say that. I told you. Don't you fucking dare.

GLORIA. You left your brother cut and bleeding, ran for the woods.

CARL. Is he dead? My brother? Is he fucking dead?

GLORIA. You're cut from the same cloth.

Bleeding the same blood.

And you ran away and left him to die.

CARL. I couldn't do nothing. I tried. I couldn't do nothing.

GLORIA. Was he asking for help? Begging you?

CARL (*holding the noose*). I'll do it, don't you fucking think I won't.

CARL *looks at his hands*.

GLORIA. This is it for you.

This is your life.

For ever.

It's never getting better.

There's only one way out of this for you.

GLORIA *stands to leave*.

You needs to put yourself out to die.

GLORIA *hums 'Que Sera, Sera'*.

*She watches* CARL *set up the noose*.

CARL *recites, simultaneously as* GLORIA *hums*.

CARL (*reciting through to the end of the scene*).
Now this is the Law of the Jungle –
as old and as true as the sky;
And the Wolf that shall keep it may prosper,
but the Wolf that shall break it must die.

As the creeper that girdles the tree-trunk
the Law runneth forward and back –
For the strength of the Pack is the Wolf,
and the strength of the Wolf is the Pack.

GLORIA *turns and leaves, humming as she exits.*

Lair-Right is the right of the Mother.
From all of her year she may claim
One haunch of each kill for her litter,
and none may deny her the same.


## Scene Eleven

*A week later.*

*The allotment.*

*Morning.*

MICHAEL *sat, wrapped in blanket on deckchair.*

*Drinking tea from* GLORIA*'s flask.*

GLORIA *stood up digging.*

GLORIA. This soil's like clay.

MICHAEL. Needs some grit or some heavy-grain sand.

GLORIA. You know what, son. You're right. What this soil
needs is some heavy-duty grit.

*Offstage we hear a football bouncing.*

MICHAEL *reacts.*

*Offstage something happens that makes it clear the ball
bounce is not* CARL *(for example, kids shouting and
laughing).*

GLORIA *carries on digging.*

And I'll tell you something else. Once we got that grit dug in. I'm gonna get us some begonias.

Yellow ones.

MICHAEL. They looks like shit.

GLORIA. You looks like shit.

MICHAEL. *You* looks like shit.

GLORIA. Pink ones, that's what I'll get...

*Fade to black.*

*The End.*

**A Nick Hern Book**

*Before It Rains* first published in Great Britain as a paperback original in 2012 by Nick Hern Books Limited, The Glasshouse, 49a Goldhawk Road, London W12 8QP, in association with Bristol Old Vic and Sherman Cymru, Cardiff

Cover image design: Smith & Milton, Bristol
Cover design: Ned Hoste, 2H

Typeset by Nick Hern Books, London
Printed and bound in Great Britain by Mimeo Ltd, Huntingdon, Cambridgeshire PE29 6XX

A CIP catalogue record for this book is available from the British Library

ISBN   978 1 84842 286 5